MW01204435

I Wish I'd Known That!

By Beth Caldwell

Secrets to Success in Business from Women Who've Been There

"Every woman business owner needs to purchase this book and read it cover to cover. The insights and lessons learned are note-worthy and time saving!" – **Michelle R. Donovan**, best selling author of "*The 29% Solution: 52 Weekly Networking Success Strategies*".

A must read - from a savvy, sophisticated, professional business woman! **Nancy Brooks**, Author of *DreamScapes: An Inspirational Guide to Your Dreams,* and International Publishing, Marketing and Sales Consultant for Entrepreneurs

In this easy-to-read resource guide, Beth Caldwell offers practical, realistic tips for starting, maintaining and growing a business. Packed with personal examples from her own diverse experiences and sharing those of other business women, Caldwell offers readers simple, sound advice with an emphasis on success. **- Carole J. Obley Spiritual Medium and Author,** *I'm Still With You: True Stories of Healing Grief Through Spirit Communication*

Beth Caldwell's book, I Wish I'd Known That, Secrets to Success in Business is an insightful book, an intimate profound companion for any woman who aspires to own her own business. Beth lays out the landscape and explains with unflinching honesty the plateaus and pitfalls that lie ahead. Never before have the myths, realities and opportunities been examined with so much vigor and pure common sense. A must read for any woman who is ready to stop struggling to reach the top rung of the ladder and instead, own her own.—**Eleanor Schano,** TV Broadcast Journalist and host of Live Well, Live Long, Speaker, and author of *Riding The Airwaves.*

Talk about spirit! I marvel on how this woman's life has abundantly unraveled! Beth is an individual who clearly demonstrates that SHE is the master of her destiny. Beth has had many obstacles to endure on her path starting at a very young age, and determined enough to embrace whatever good she could create out of each situation as an opportunity to grow. All women should be reading this book because if there is a seed that needs to be a flourishing plant, it is Beth Caldwell! —**Grace Cardona**, Business Owner, Graceful Expressions, Dubai.

Secrets to Success in Business

Dedication

To my mom, Kathy Lugaila, who always believed me when I told her I was going to grow up and write a book, own a business, be on TV and own a magazine. Thanks for believing in me.

Secrets to Success in Business

Acknowledgements

Growing up, my role models were different than those of my friends. They admired models and rock stars and I wanted to be Ann Marie from That Girl, Mary Tyler Moore, Jamie Sommers, the Bionic Woman, Lynda Carter, Wonder Woman, and later Connie Selleca, when she played a flight attendant on the TV Series Flying High.

All of my role models were independent single career women, and looking back, I have spent parts of my career in advertising, entertainment, teaching, reporting, and even a brief time working for the airlines. As I became older and was raising children, I realized that the women who have most influenced my life were my aunts Margie, Lois, and Candace. The three of them had a profound effect on my life. All of them are successful parents, community members, and career women, and they all enjoy committed marriages. Often when faced with an issue, I think of what my aunts would do, and when things get crazy and hectic, I remember my aunt Lois, her kids, her pets, her station wagon, and her cups of tea and realize that life is exactly the way I want it.

Beth Caldwell

Learn from the mistakes of others. You can't live
long enough to make them all yourself.
Eleanor Roosevelt

Foreword

Nancy Brooks, Author of **DreamScapes:
An Inspirational Guide to Your Dreams,**
and International Publishing, Marketing and
Sales Consultant for Entrepreneurs

Creating a business is like being a first time parent –
your baby doesn't come with a specified blueprint. Just
advice from friends and family with no guarantee that
they know what they're doing either. Learning as we go is
often painful and expensive.

Creating a successful business can be similar. Who do
we trust with our "baby business", its mission statement
and our resources? How do you discover the wisdom and
knowledge (specific to your product or service) that is
timeless and also contemporary in the current market-
place? And when do you seek advice from professionals?

**I Wish I'd Known That! Secrets To Success In
Business** is a blueprint that challenges the business
owner to clarify their purpose, resources and market. Author, Beth Caldwell, leads us through a *"new business check
list*, educating, supporting and inspiring would-be entrepreneurs to do it right the first time! And for those of us
already in an established business, the **"Secrets to Success"** shows us where we've hit the mark and where we
can improve our image and increase our financial income.

A must read - from a savvy, sophisticated, professional
business woman!

Nancy Brooks

Table of Contents

Table of Contents

Great ideas can come from unexpected places,
and the best ideas don't necessarily come from
high priced marketing firms.
Cheryl Andonian
Polliwalks, Inc.
Newburyport, MA

Chapter One

Name Your Business

For some people, naming their business is the easiest part of starting their business. For others, it is a   painstaking, long process riddled with research, data, opinions and input. When I began my Public Relations business, it happened so fast I didn't have time for an official name. I'm known to act first and research later, not something I   recommend, especially in business planning.

Consider pizza chains where you have names that range from Pizza Uno to Pizza Schmizza. Before Google, having a name in the first part of the alphabet was very important, so you could be found first in the yellow pages. Today, Domino's Pizza is the second largest franchised pizza chain in the United States. Originally named Dominick's, the Michigan business was sold to brothers Tom and James Monoghan in the 1960's for $575.00. A few years later, Tom bought his brothers share of the business with a second-hand car, and renamed the shop, **Domino's**. It's hard to imagine Dominick's Pizza as an international pizza chain, but Domino's makes sense. Why? Who knows.

While doing research for this book, I interviewed hundreds of small businesses, many of them with very plain jane names, many with very interesting names and some with unusual and unpronounceable names.

For example, Kristen Goede is the founder of **Objets d'Envy**, handcrafted crystal-lux jewelry that is carried in boutiques across the Midwest. Kristen's advice, "Be absolutely sure your business name is easy to spell and pronounceable. I love my company name and there's a great story behind it. But, it's French and most people can't spell or pronounce it. The French concept works for me, because I'm in the fashion industry, but I wouldn't do it again." Her problem: Kristen is a wholesaler of fashionable and stunning Swarovski Crystal jewelry. Her ideal clients are unique boutiques and trendy fashion stores, and they need to be able to find her easily. Unless they know her personally, its going to be tough for them to locate her. If they do recall her name, its easy to misspell. Objets D' Envy looks trendy on a gift box or a shopping bag, but doesn't make her any money if she can't be found by her ideal clients. Kristen wisely kept her name, but has added a second website called **Modern Sparkle**, a perfect fit for the type of jewelry she designs, easily found and remembered, and she has loaded the website with key words and phrases that wholesalers would type into search engines. A fashionable and smart save for her business.

Poliwalks is very successful startup business with a great name. Owner Cheryl Andonian shares this story: "We were brainstorming about what our brand name should be— something to really capture our animal themed "footprinting" waterproof shoes for kids. We were tossing ideas around out loud...Frogs, Frogz, Toads, Polliwogs, and in an AHA moment my then ten year old son declared, "I know, **POLLIWALKS!**"

It captured everything that we wanted to say about our brand in one word. We trademarked and reached one million in sales within our first year. I guess the lesson here is that great ideas can come from unexpected places and that the best ideas don't necessarily come from high priced marketing firms."

A friend of mine, Bonnie Budzowski had a name problem. She is an author, speaker and coach who works with people who want to become published in order to increase their credibility. She originally started her business as The Word Coach, a very clever name, but most people didn't get the concept. People assumed she was an editor or a tutor. Frustrated, she hired a coach to revamp her message and now calls her company **InCredible Messages**. Keeping people credible in their work is very important to her, and it's a fantastic play on words. Bonnie doesn't just help people write books, she helps with all written and verbal messages including email, reports, letters, articles, pamphlets, booklets, etc. She helps professionals make their written works compelling and incredible. Another great save.

Here's a rule breaker for you— **Carabella** is a fashionable clothing store for women in Oakmont, PA. People assume that this is a well known Italian phrase meaning "dear beauty", or "beautiful face" in Spanish. However, the name came about when the owner, Carol Kinkela wrote out the names of her family members while brainstorming for a business name. Carabella includes the initials for her, her husband and her two sons. This beautiful name with a dual meaning been very successful for her.

Less than 5% of the business owners that I interviewed consulted with an agency or a branding company to select their name and image. I don't think it's a bad idea to consult with a branding agency, I just think that entrepreneurs tend to be creative and come up with their own ideas, and, the idea of branding is still somewhat new to small business owners. Branding agencies can charge up to $50,000. If you are building a national restaurant chain, it's a necessary step, but for the typical small business owner, it's not affordable.

Business owners who are the most satisfied with their names have names that completely and concisely say exactly what they do. 2007 International Coach of the Year Mark Simple has a unique niche coaching business. **Successful Together** works with women in home based business who need more support from their spouse. Mark comments, "I wanted a business name that reflected my purpose and passion as a coach and I'm very happy with this name. It concisely describes who I am and what I do."

Be sure that the name you choose will not be misunderstood for a completely different field. For example, **Regus**, the company where I rent my office suite is often mistaken for **Regis Salons**. Regus offers fully equipped and staffed business centers and executive offices that meet the needs of unique businesses in over 750 worldwide locations. It's a brilliant idea for large companies that have remote locations, as well as ideal for entrepreneurs and independent contractors.

Recently, businesses that have suffered a crisis or natural disaster have been able to move right into a fully equipped and staffed office and not miss a day of work while waiting for repairs, insurance reimbursements, etc.

British entrepreneur Mark Dixon opened the first Regus Business Center in Brussels, Belgium in 1989. Regis Hair Salon began in the small town of Edina, Minnesota in 1958, when Myron Kunin took over his parents beauty salons and moved them from department stores into strip malls. Through a number of buyouts and acquisitions, Regis Corporation has over 13,500 worldwide locations. One began in the United States and moved overseas, the other began in Europe and moved overseas. It probably never occurred to either man that they'd ever be mistaken for the other. Though their name has not been changed, Regus' marketing materials are now clearly branded with the more identifiable business works words "office", "business", "businessworld", and "business center".

It's unlikely that either entrepreneur could have ever foreseen this situation. However, Julie Dana, Home Stylist from Buffalo, NY wishes she had put some more thought into her business name, **The Home Stylist**. Julie is an expert in home staging but people often ask her if she is a hair stylist who works from home. Julie says, "I am personable and outgoing, so I don't mind if people ask me to explain what I do. It gives me a reason to talk with them. Still, it never occurred to me that people would think that I did hair."

Your business name is crucially important to your overall success and marketing strategy. It deserves some thought and some planning. I recommend that you start out with the right name, rather than have to make changes, add websites and re-print business cards and marketing materials.

When it comes to your business name, I don't want you saying, "I wish I'd known that was a bad choice for a name". You can change your name, reprint your marketing materials, etc, but take the time to think through this important decision. Here are some key questions to answer before making your decision:

Questions To Ask Before
Naming Your Business:

1. Does the name describe who you are and what you do?
2. Is the name easy to pronounce and spell?
3. Is the name legally available in your state?
4. Is the website URL available?
5. If industry should change, or you should decide to add or change services in the future, expand your services to other states or become international, would this name still work?
6. Does your name clearly identify what you do or can it be misunderstood for something else? This is something to be aware of because to some people their name makes total sense, but to an outsider the name may have a completely different meaning. If your ideal clients get it, and you love it, go for it!

Sometimes we both wonder if we should have borrowed
the start up funds. We would have had more funds for
marketing and advertising. Using our own money
has limited our ability to market widely.

Tangela Walker-Craft
Simply   Necessary, Inc.
Lakeland, Florida

Chapter Two

Borrowing Money

The majority of small businesses use some type of financing. In my research I came across a variety of types of financing and lots of creativity. There are a number of resources to assist the small business owner in creating a business plan and an estimate of startup and business costs. How and when to borrow money is a personal choice, but don't let your enthusiasm for your new venture cloud your judgment.

If you have no startup funds, carefully consider keeping your day job while you begin to build your new business, especially if you are planning on using a home equity loan or credit cards to finance your startup costs.

Before borrowing money, consult an expert to determine a good estimate of your startup costs, your initial business investment, and most importantly your break even point. Realize that you may not begin seeing a profit immediately, so consider borrowing enough to get you past your break even point, in case of unforeseen circumstances.

Over 40% of the businesses that I interviewed started their business with personal money, home equity loans, family loans, or credit cards. Usually it was the quickest and easiest way to start.

After being in business for 2 years, many were able to apply for SBA loans to pay off their second mortgages or credit lines and begin to establish credit in their business name.

Having sufficient capital is one of the most important components to having a successful business. There are always exceptions, but having enough money is always much better than struggling to make ends meet. Have you noticed how a crisis never seems to happen when you have money in the bank?

If you're not comfortable taking the risk with a home equity loan, or paying high interest credit card loans, there are a few other options:

- Credit Unions
- Family Loans
- Signature Loans
- Community Express Loan Program
- Venture Capitalist
- Angel Investors
- Traditional Bank Loans or SBA Backed Loans
- Personal Savings
- SBIC (Small Business Investment Company)
- Employee Stock Ownership (ESOP)
- Short term or Long Term Business Loans
- Microloans
- Private Investors
- Personal Line of Credit (usually secured)
- Community Loan Programs
- Business Alliance
- Sale of Personal Assets
  (2nd home boat, 2nd car, Investments, etc.)

Borrowing money is not easy, especially for a startup business. If you are new to your business, banks will often insist on a personal guarantee as well as equity. This is a burden for most small business owners.

SBA Business Loans help to guarantee longer term loans. Many SBA Loans are declined, but the reason for the declines are most often poor preparation of the paperwork. If you prefer to fund your business with a business loan rather than a home equity loan, prepare your paperwork meticulously. Remember, its not personal to the bank. They make money from loans. In order to approve your loan, they want to be certain that you have done your homework, have business experience in your field, and are very aware of your business plan, your assets and liabilities and your financial forecast. There are many resources to assist you in preparing the paperwork, which you can find online or at your local Small Business Development Center.

An impressive product created by Sue Malone and her partner Tom Jochner is the ***Community Express Loan Program,*** where almost any entrepreneur can get an SBA-backed $25K loan within one week after filling out a one page form. The loan program was a product of Sue's frustration for small business owners. Sue says, "I went to the SBA and I said you are not doing anything for small businesses. They pointed me to their microloan program. I looked into it and found they had done **seven** loans. No one could meet the requirements. I said something has got to change. So I started this program. Just about anyone can come to me. For more information, visit her website: www.StrategiesForSmallBusiness.com.

When borrowing money, I encourage you to consider the following expenses, and retain enough funds to cover up to two years, depending on your break-even point. Here are items often left out on a financial plan that can really add up:

- Advertising
- Public or community relations
- Graphic and website design
- Membership in professional organizations & chambers
- Networking events
- Professional publications and subscriptions
- Business cards, postage, stationery & signage
- Professional licenses or permits
- Credit card fees
- Business account setup fees
- Fictitious name registration
- Professional services such as a virtual assistant, legal services, bookkeeping, etc.
- Business insurance
- Membership in the Better Business Bureau
- Virtual address or PO box for a home based business

Don't wait until you are at a profit level to purchase these services. I broke a lot of traditional rules when starting my business. If there is one thing that I wish I'd done differently it's that I wish I'd joined my local chamber of commerce immediately. I kept putting it off until I could afford it, and I regret that.

Becoming affiliated with a chamber has many benefits. For your clients, it gives you instant credibility. Recent studies show that being affiliated with a chamber of commerce gives customers the same reassurances as being a part of the BBB. It shows you have investment in the community. For your business, membership gives you networking opportunities, educational workshops and a support system of other business owners. So get involved, it's a great idea!

A new national study reveals that membership in a   local chamber of commerce can significantly boost a business's image among consumers, as well as among other businesses. In a scientific survey of 2000 U.S. adults, The Schapiro Group, an Atlanta-based strategic consulting firm, found positive perceptions of chamber members in a number of areas, including overall   favorability, consumer awareness and reputation, and likelihood of future patronage.

—The Schapiro Group, August, 2007

The biggest reason I took the plunge and moved into an office was that being able to actually work at home was unpredictable, between my animals and other interruptions. I was also really tired of meeting clients at Starbucks. It's definitely a struggle some months but I feel it's really worth it. I still do some work at home, including my billing, but when I'm at the office I get a lot more done.

Jane E. Tate, Attorney
Kailua, Hawaii

Chapter Three

Your Office Location

I am a trend-setter when it comes to office location. In 1992, I was the first person in my neighborhood to have a computer in my home. I was a travel agent with a one year old and expecting my second child. At the time, the travel industry paid great commissions and I had a nice clientele built up. I did group travel, business and some vacations from home during my sons nap time and for an hour or two after dinner. I loved working at home and continued to do so for seventeen years and several career changes. In September 2008, I relocated my home based Public Relations business into a beautiful executive suite on the third floor of a building in a professional office park. As I notice more and more people leaving corporate jobs to work from home, I'm on my way back to the office and I love it.

Choosing your office is a very personal decision. For me, it affected just me and my family. You may have staff to consider. There are pros and cons to working from home or renting an office. The biggest drawback of renting an office is probably the expense. The biggest advantage is the boost in your professional image. The day I moved into my new office, I gained two big clients. Was it an affirmation of my making the right choice, or did I suddenly have the confidence to attract new clients?

When choosing an office location, consider the following:

- Does it make sense to move into an office at this time, or can you easily work from a home office? Virtual Assistants, Graphic Designers, Web Designers, Internet Based Businesses, even Attorneys and Architects can work from a home office.
- If you are in a home office do you have a professional place to meet with your clients?
- Can you share an office space with a fellow consultant? Can you barter for an empty office space one or two days per month for meetings?
- If renting an office, never sign more than a twelve month lease. Get a six month lease if you can. You want to be able to move easily if you should happen to get a bad neighbor, or if your business should grow so fast that you need more space.
- Is your location easy to find and offer parking for your clients?
- Obviously if you are a bridal shop, retail store or a day spa you want to be in a high traffic area on the ground floor. Consultants, coaches, and graphic or web designers can be housed in a more remote area.
- Is there a conference or meeting room available?
- Is signage permitted to promote your business?
- Is the office hard wired for your equipment?
- Are services such as long distance, Wi-Fi, secure internet, fax line, etc. available with the rent or for an additional fee?
- How are noisy or messy tenants dealt with?

If you're not sure about getting an office, but really want a professional location, I highly recommend short term executive office suites such as **Intelligent Office**, **Offices2Share**, **Regus**, or **Your Office**. Check with your local business development center or chamber of commerce to find local sources for short term affordable office rentals. Do a Google search in your area for "Virtual Office", "Business Incubator" or "Executive Suites".

If you can substantiate the reason for moving, and can find a suitable space that allows for even more growth at an affordable price, you can build your empire in a classy space that can make you even more productive and consequently more profitable.

Norma J. Rist & Katrina Z. Jones
Small Business Savvy

Price elasticity is far greater than most people realize. I would advise never to set prices based on the rates of   competitors. How do you know they're making any money?
Lori Saitz
Zen Rabbit Baking Company
Palm Beach Gardens, Florida

Chapter Four

Setting Your Prices

Libraries of books have been written on this subject. Traditionally women undercharge for their services and under value their expertise compared to men.

I interviewed dozens of female business owners on this subject and have made several mistakes myself in this area.

There are several mistakes that business owners make when setting their prices:

- Setting prices too high
- Setting prices too low
- Not appreciating the value of your services
- Giving away services
- Feeling guilty for being paid what you're worth

I have worked with businesswomen who charge just enough to cover their costs and I have mentored business women who have no business because they are charging outrageous and unreasonable fees that are not in line with their services. This is the same mistake that people make when selling their homes based on how much they want to profit. This model doesn't work in the housing market or the business market. Setting prices too high can be as bad as setting them too low.

When people ask me if they should lower prices in   order to gain a competitive edge, I always answer the same. I don't recommend discounting your prices, instead, I recommend increasing your value. Adding value to your service is preferable, especially if your additional value does not come out of your profits. One of the things that I do to add value to my clients is a weekly reporting on their account, in addition to the monthly meeting we have. Once a week I review their goals, what steps we have made to reach them, and what we're planning for the upcoming week. It takes me less than five minutes, makes them feel confident that I'm on top of their media and publicity goals, and frees them up to focus on other aspects of their businesses.

Take some time to think of how you can add value and go the extra mile for your clients. What can you offer that no one else can? If you can't think of anything right now, list all the reasons why you are the best business in your field. You don't have to include every reason in your company brochure, but it will help you in feeling confident about your fees. Keep this information in your journal and review it often. It will help you to keep up your confidence as well as see your progress as you develop additional skills.

The best thing you can do for your business income is regularly review your profit and loss statement, and adjust accordingly. I highly recommend you begin monthly accounting, rather than quarterly or annual accounting. It really helps to keep track of your income and expenses. Not only will you realize how much you're earning, you will also recognize and correct errors easily, and be able to take more advantage of deductions and write offs. when you keep a close tab on your books. When you just visit your accountant once a year, you can't possibly remember every business expense, and you lose valuable deductions that way.

Be sure to consider all possible costs when setting your fees. Delivery fees, shipping, paper, presentation folders, phone calls, faxes, credit card processing fees, thank you gifts and your office overhead all need to be counted into your profit and loss.

If you have an inventory, be sure that you know the difference between your markup and your margin. Some businesses get into trouble by offering a discount that is equal to or greater than their margin, essentially losing money on a sale. This is another reason to never offer a discount. If you want to offer a special on your inventory, give a gift with purchase rather than a discount your product.

If you offer a service, determine if you will charge hourly or by the project. It's perfectly fine to have more than one option, and a great idea to have packages to offer, especially if you offer services. This allows you to showcase all of your services and often will allow you to retain clients for a longer period of time.

Setting your prices can be one of the most challenging aspects to your business, and one that you need to give a lot of thought and preparation to. I recommend that you review your fees with your bookkeeper annually or more often if you are stocking and selling an   inventory.

If you are providing a service, there is a range of fees and services that are typical for your industry as well as your region. Begin here and carefully consider your differences from your competition, the value that you have to offer and the advantages to doing business with you. You must also consider the costs involved in doing business, and don't forget to include your time.

When setting the prices for my public relations business, I made the mistake of not considering the time I spent in preparing to meet with a client, research and development for individual publicity campaigns, or the time that it takes to meet with clients or discuss strategies during the month. I immediately realized that I was spending a lot more time on projects than I was billing for. Fortunately, I became aware this early and was able to adjust my fees for new clients. I still offer hourly fees for some projects, but now I most often bill per project, because its difficult for me to time my creativity.

Once you set your prices, don't justify your fees or apologize for them. I can give you good advice and share tips and techniques, but I can't give you confidence. You must believe that you are worth what you're charging. If you explain or apologize for your fees, people are not going to want to pay you.

Remind yourself frequently of your value. The more you believe in yourself, the easier this will become. Don't hesitate to ask for and keep testimonials and thank you notes from current and former clients. In fact, ask them to share specifically how you helped them. It's a fantastic idea to share testimonials on your website and in your marketing materials, and it also gives a little publicity to the client. Note: if you are someone who needs to keep your clients information confidential; you can still use testimonials, just use their initials, first name, or description. For example a tutor could use this name on a testimonial: —Susie J., Mom of a 2nd grader.

Finally, make it easy for clients to pay you. Offer packages, payment options, auto payments, and accept credit cards. The cost of your credit card processing is a part of doing business.

Ten Tips for Setting Your Prices

- Have a financial policy, know your rates, your forms of payments, and policies on accepting checks and credit cards. Also have a policy just in case you have to deal with late payments or bad checks.

- Know the clients that you want to work with, and seek them out. Don't seek clients who cannot afford you. Once you are established, you can always volunteer or take an occasional pro-bono client.

- Don't be afraid to make an adjustment in your fees if you realize you've made an error.

- Never be afraid to expect payment in advance. Often women will invoice for services and then wait to be paid. Remember you are in business, so act like it!

- Don't offer discounts, but DO offer **EXCEPTIONAL VALUE!**

- Review your fees regularly

- Don't accept clients who cannot afford you unless you can afford to work as a volunteer

- Know how much you are making

- **REMEMBER YOUR VALUE!**

- **GET PAID WHAT YOU"RE WORTH!**

Right or wrong, people value what they pay for.
When you increase the price of your products or services,
people believe they are worth more. We know this is not
always true, but the PERCEPTION is that it must be a great
service if it is expensive. What does your price say about your
service? Could you command more respect if you
increased your price?

**Mikelann Valterra, author of
Why Women Earn Less—How to Make
What You're Really Worth
Seattle, Washington**

I'm in a service-based business and my website is
absolutely critical to my success. I think the same is
true for a product based business. Either way, a website
is such a simple thing to obtain now that there isn't an
excuse not to have one.

Alyssa Lang
Hybrid Photography
El Cajon, California

Chapter Five

Creating Your Web Presence

It's my opinion that a website is the most important tool available to you, to promote yourself or your business. Not only are websites more affordable than they have ever been, more people than ever go to the internet first when seeking a product or a service.

As a publicist I insist that my clients have a website. When I say website, I mean a **<u>real</u>** website meant for business, not a MySpace page, not a LinkedIn profile, not a FaceBook account or a free website with ads all over it.

You need a real website that looks professional. It doesn't have to be fancy, just tell what you do, why you're great, and how to hire you.

I teach a popular workshop on marketing and PR called **"Am I Googleable?"** One of the components of this workshop is helping business professionals to create or improve their websites so that they are friendly to the media, as well as potential clients.

I refer to websites as your "online business card" or your online storefront. When shopping for a designer, pretend that you are hiring a professional interior designer for your brick and mortar store.

If you are starting from scratch, begin by doing some online research. Spend some time looking at several websites taking note of the ones that you really like and ones that you don't care for. Begin looking in your own industry and branch out from there.

When you are looking at websites and you come across one that is designed in a way that interests you, scroll down to the very bottom of the page, and often you will find a link that says "website designed and maintained by: _____." You can usually click on this link which will take you to that designer, and usually they will have samples of their work there.

To create your online presence, you need to make three key purchases:

1. Your domain name
2. Your website hosting
3. Your website design

The domain name, also called your URL, is your website address (www.**yourcompanyname**.com). The hosting is the process of taking your website and making it "live" and available on the internet. The design is the content that's placed on your site. You can purchase these items individually on your own, or have your web designer handle this for you.

Your domain name is very important and needs to be one that is easily spelled and remembered. I recommend that you get several web addresses, and have them all point to your main URL (WWW) address. For example, if you are a small company that manufactures ceiling fans in Toledo, Ohio, you will probably want the name of your company as your primary web address and will use it on all of your marketing materials:

www.TheCeilingFanCompany.com

People who know you by your business name will find you easily online. But what about someone who just moved to Toledo and needs a new ceiling fan? They don't know your company name, so they are going to go to a website search and type:

ceiling fan Toledo

Is your company going to come up first in their web search? You have a better chance of them finding you if you also have these domain names:

www.ToledoCeilingFanCompany.com
and
www.ToledoCeilingFans.com

In addition to retailing ceiling fans, you also wholesale to large lighting and home stores across the US and Canada. Current clients who purchase from you already know who you are, but what about potential new clients?

www.WholesaleCeilingFans.com
www.CeilingFans4Sale.com

These are not each individual websites, they are individual URL address that each point to your main website. You do not have to pay hosting for these URL's, just for the domain names, which range in price of $1.99-$15.00 per year.

While you are buying URL's, go ahead and purchase yourownname.com. Its not unusual for people to search for your business by your first and last name.

If you have a name that is easily misspelled, then purchase the commonly misspelled version also. Make it easy for people to find you.

I am often asked if it is ok to get a .NET address or a .BIZ address? My answer is that people still prefer a .COM address, so try and get a .COM address if you can. Get creative by adding hyphens like www.hope-counseling-services.com. When you use your web link in an online ad or in your email signature or e-newsletter, it doesn't matter if there are hyphens because people are clicking right through to your site.

In addition to hyphens, check to see if your company name is available with the words *my*, *your*, or *the* in front of it like w w w . y o u r h e a l t h y j o u r n e y . c o m   o r www.thehandwritingexpert.com. Before you purchase anything with a .NET or with hyphens, do your homework and see what the .com address that is similar to yours has online. You do not want to send anyone to your competitors by accident.

If someone has a similar business to yours and already has your name at a .com website, I think you are doing nothing but generating business for them if you take the .NET or .BIZ companion site.

If you are lucky enough to get your name with a .COM, purchase the .NET also so that you own it. That will protect you from copycats and competitors trying to edge into your client base.

Hosting fees range from $4/month to $99/year. I usually purchase my hosting right along with the domain name from the same company, so that everything is in the same place. Check with your designer to see if they work with a specific company. When choosing a host, make sure they are a reputable company with a backup host that is online more than 95% of the time. If the host is down, your site is down. Most host providers now offer 24 hour support and a backup plan for power outages or emergency situations.

When you receive a notice that your domain name and hosting payments are due, do not ignore that. Pay it, and pay for it for as many months as you can get. If you are planning on staying in businesses, the last thing you want is for someone to go to your website and get a "page not found" error message. It's like saying, oops, forgot to pay my bill... I am disorganized and cluttered.

Your website is as important as your business telephone. You would never neglect to pay your phone bill, can you imagine having clients call you and getting a message "this phone is temporarily out of order" message? Everyone knows that means that you didn't pay your bill on time.

Your domain name and hosting payment are due annually. Mark it on your calendar and you won't need to worry about losing track, or overlooking the invoices.

Web design fees can range from $500-$5,000. Shopping for a web designer is as important as choosing a financial planner. Most people go on the recommendations of their business network, their chamber of commerce or from the recommendation of friends and family.

Do not hire someone who does web design as a hobby. Remember when I said that your website is your online storefront? Would you hire a "hobby" contractor to build your store front? Would you hire a part-time art student to handle your business marketing? Keep this in mind if you are tempted to hire an art student or a high school student to build your website.

In addition, make sure you have ownership of your hosting and web address, as well as complete access to your site to make updates and changes. Ideally, your website should be set up to allow you to log on and make updates and changes. If it's not, you still need to know the access information, in the case that your web designer is not available. What happens if your designer decides to go backpacking in Europe?

Letting your web designer have complete ownership and control over your website is the equivalent to letting your student intern have the keys and access codes to your brick and mortar building. At best, your site may become outdated, and at worst you'll have to start from scratch. Always have a backup copy of the text and content on your website, including the photos, so if something does happen, you can quickly and easily re create it without too much downtime. Don't be embarrassed about asking your designer to provide these files. You paid for them.

Once you have your website built, make the most of it to attract new business and new clients. Remember I said that your website is just like a real store? Imagine people visiting your website just as they walk through stores in the mall. They wander by, take a peek, you ask, "Can I help you?" and they say, "No, just looking..." and they leave. How do you get them to come back? Or...how do you get them to call you and hire you? Your website should be polished, professional, informative and not overwhelming. Even before your website is up and running have a place for people to give you their contact information so that you can keep in touch with them via your email newsletter or e-zine. Think of your website as you do your marketing and public relations. Its very important, and its always a work in progress. This is NOT something you do once and leave alone. Continually update and improve your website.

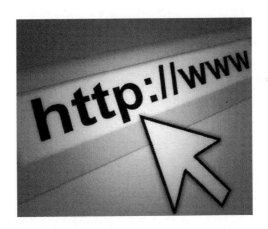

Here are some tips for an effective website:

- Visit **www.nameboy.com** to shop for website names. I like this site because it will give you alternative suggestions if your first choice is unavailable.
- If you are not certain about hosting, purchase it monthly at first, and then, when you're comfortable with a hosting service, purchase an annual plan.
- Purchase several website addresses including your own name and have them "point" or "forward" to your website.
- Learn how to make simple changes to your website and keep it updated. Its not as difficult as you probably think and it's often easier and faster for you to just go in and add the upcoming event than to write the details down for your web designer, explain what you want, have them log in and make the changes, then bill you.
- Choose a website name that is catchy and easy to remember. Put this website name on ALL of your marketing materials and add it to your email signature line with a link that will take people directly to your website.
- Make sure your contact information is easy to find on every page. Make it easy for potential clients to find you. Include physical directions if necessary.
- Add testimonials to your website whenever possible, and add new testimonials on a regular basis.
- Don't give too much information, they need to have a reason to call you.
- Have updated and professional photos of you and your staff. People like to see who they are doing business with.

- Have links to your website available on all of your social networking sites.
- Collect the names and contact information of people who visit your site. This is easy to do if you offer a free report or a complimentary subscription to your e-zine.

An effective website can lead to increased revenues, so get online!

"Connecting with people who have more influence and success raises your skill level and creates new opportunities for you."
Sandra Yancey
Founder and President of eWomen Network
Dallas, Texas

Chapter Six

Joining Professional Organizations

This is my personal biggest "I Wish I'd Known That". I wish I had joined my local chamber of commerce when I first started my business, rather than waiting. It's crucial to network with other business owners, and I highly recommend your local chamber to begin with. If you are borrowing money to begin your business, borrow enough money to pay your first year dues and membership fees for several organizations. I don't want you to miss the educational, networking and mentoring benefits because you don't have the money. If you have more than one chamber in your area, most will let you attend events as a non member, so you can visit before joining.

Besides joining your local chamber, there are other organizations you should consider belonging to. Professional Organizers have NAPO, the National Association of Professional Organizers. Physicians, Chiropractors, Nutritionists, Coaches, Financial Planners, Professional Care Givers and even day care centers have state, regional or national organizations that can accredit them, or just give them a level of professionalism that the general public trusts.

Chambers of Commerce give you local credibility as well as networking and educational opportunities. Many chamber members prefer to do business with other chamber members, so being listed in their directory can be very helpful.

Networking groups give you the opportunity to network with other professionals. There are a variety of networking groups so you may want to visit before joining. Some groups are very serious and structured, while others are more socially oriented.

When attending a networking meeting, it's important to realize that you are NOT going there to sell. You are going to make connections. This is a big source of frustration with many networking organizations. Take the advice of **Michelle Donovan**, author of **The 29% Solution**, "Successful networking is about learning how to work the process, its not "net-SIT" or "net-EAT" , its not something that you can just let happen." Michelle's book offers 52 weekly networking strategies to help you establish real connections through networking.

It can be tempting to attend as many networking events as you are able, but you must keep it balanced. **Jill Lublin**, author of **Guerilla Publicity** & **Get Noticed Get Referrals** recommends limiting yourself to four networking events per month. If four is too much for you then limit yourself to two. Often I am invited to several events in the same month and I really want to attend all of them. When this happens, I go back to Jill's rule and I choose four. I realize that many people are not as outgoing, or do not have flexible work schedules, and for these people it's hard to fit even two events into a month. I think this is a mistake.

Take the advice of **Fabienne Frederickson**, a woman whose advice greatly impacted my personal businesses. Fabienne is the creator of **Client Attraction**, and she recommends that you build networking into your marketing plan by spending one day a week marketing your business. (Did you notice that recommendation comes from THREE very successful women? I meant to repeat that!) If you don't think it's possible for you to network weekly, then visit Fabienne's website to get her free CD on the subject. You can find it at ClientAttraction.com.

The most difficult part of a marketing plan is getting started, and once you make a plan, this will become easier. (We'll get to this in chapters 8 and 9)

It's a good idea to attend a networking event with a goal to meet two new business connections. If you attend with the purpose of trying to connect with everyone in attendance, you will appear aggressive, and pushy. Take time to greet and talk to other business owners in an unhurried fashion, and show genuine interest in others and what they have to offer. A good connection would be someone that you plan to meet with again over coffee in order to learn more about one another with the intention to refer business to each other, or to do "eventworking" together.

Making the Most of Networking and Professional Memberships:

- Add the logos of your membership organizations to your website and marketing materials.
- Always attend events prepared with business cards, brochures, flyers or announcements and have your 10-30 second commercial ready.
- If you are running late for an event, take a moment to relax before entering. Take a few deep breaths, remind yourself why you are attending, and put a smile on your face. The office will survive while you're away.
- When someone hands you a business card, look directly at it and comment. If you can't think of anything positive to say, you can always say "Isn't that interesting."
- If someone is monopolizing your time, or if you feel that you are talking to someone who isn't interested in connecting with you, just say, "It's been very nice chatting with you, but I hate to monopolize your time."
- Don't expect to attend networking events and sell your products or services on the spot. If someone tells you they want to do business with you, that's a genuine bonus.
- Be genuine in your effort to help others in business. Let them know how you can help them and you can help one another.
- When attending professional workshops, be gracious to the planner and the presenter. Don't seek them out immediately after the event with complaints. Appreciate the time and effort that it takes to plan events and run trainings.

- If you attend a meeting with a dull speaker, or you are at a presentation that is reviewing information you already know, try to learn something new, or meet someone new to network with. If the subject becomes tedious, quietly review paperwork, go over your goals or to do list, or be discreet and work on something else until the next presenter begins.

Membership fees, workshop attendance and networking events are necessary to the success of your business. These events can be deductable and you should save your receipts and turn them into your book keeper monthly.

Expert Tip:
I like to arrive at events 15 to 20 minutes early.
Frequently, they are still setting up and I can identify the movers and shakers and those who are putting on the event.
They can introduce you to important people when they arrive, before others try to monopolize them.
Jill Lublin, Speaker and Author Guerilla Publicity, and Get Noticed Get Referrals.

Opportunities to network vary in different regions. Here is a list of popular networking organizations:

- BNI (Business Networking International)
- BPW (Business & Professional Women)
- Downtown Women's Club (DWC)
- eWomen Network (my personal favorite)
- Joy of Connecting (JOC)
- NAWBO (The National Organization of Women Business Owners)
- Your local Chamber of Commerce or Business Development Resource Center

A Note About Social Networking

Web-based social networking sites such as LinkedIn®, Facebook, Plaxo, and Twitter and the various blogging opportunities should be used as an enhancement, not a replacement for professional business memberships and affiliations. Social networking is powerful and can greatly impact your business.

Depending on your target market and your product, you may be able to significantly increase your exposure by embracing social networking. Take the time to learn how to use it smartly because businesses of all sizes are jumping on this wave and riding it to the bank.

If you are operating on a shoestring budget, then this is a form of advertising and marketing that is free, well within your budget. However, unless you are a web-based sales or information based business, you will need to compliment your social networking with traditional networking.

You know the saying — people do businesses with those they know, like and trust!

Happy networking!

You can't make money if your are crazy busy all the time. If you are doing everything, then all you have time for is the urgent and unimportant. You have to have time to be doing the things that are important in your business, not just the urgent.

Jim Merante
Padgett Business Services
Murrysville, Pennsylvania

Chapter Seven

Hiring Staff

Growing your business to include staff is a fantastic sign that your business is growing. It's very important to recognize exactly when you're ready to hire and also recognize when its not quite time yet.

It's critical to your success that you have the right staff surrounding you, supporting you and who will eventually be able to run the business in your absence.

Hiring staff to support you is a huge step. For some companies this can greatly increase your expenses, and its not a decision to be made lightly. The positive side is that as an entrepreneur, your income is limited to the number of hours in the day. Having help will increase your expenses but done right will also increase your income.

Depending on the type of business you have, you may be able to outsource some support, and for many, this is their first step in growth. My business is extremely busy during peak times of the year and at other times things can really slow down. It doesn't make sense for me to hire a staff to support me because I couldn't   afford to pay them during the slow months. For me, outsourcing is the best choice. I outsource bookkeeping, accounting, my own marketing and public relations (even the publicist needs a publicist) ,small jobs such as blogging and writing web copy. My office suite through Regus provides a very professional office staff, including a receptionist (luv ya Lynne) who answers calls, and a professional office staff (Tymra and Leesha) who handle incoming and outgoing mail, faxes, projects, and many other tasks that make me look very professional and pulled together. I sub-contract to an experienced, professional marketing and PR consultant who wants to work part-time at this stage of her life. She helps me out during busy times and can take over for me in a pinch if I become sick or need to travel.

Outsourcing works well for me. Some businesses prefer staff that is 100% devoted. In that case, outsourcing won't work. If you're not ready to hire yet, consider trying an intern or hiring a temp. It's a good way to ease into becoming a "boss."

Before hiring, in fact before interviewing, you need to have some employee and human resource systems in place. Before taking on staff, your business needs to be legal and formally on paper. An attorney can help you decide if you need to incorporate.

By this time you should already have your Employer Identification Number (EIN) from the IRS, as well as a business banking account titled in your business name. You will want to have the appropriate business insurance to protect yourself and your business from potential liabilities. You will also need an employee manual, payroll system and policies and procedures for wages, hiring, firing, sick time, benefits, security issues, etc. You can spend time researching compliance issues, or out-source your human resource needs to a qualified Professional Human Resource Professional. If you are a beginner to employment law, I guarantee you will find out that you are now responsible for things that have never before occurred to you.

We are probably all competent enough to write out and establish our own procedures. However, I think that our businesses are better served when we to spend our hours on what we're good at, and let others grow in their business by hiring them to cover those areas that they specialize in.

Employment laws change often, and vary in states and municipalities, so when it comes to HR policies I prefer to leave these details to the experts who are well qualified to keep my business legal and efficiently operating.

You should have an attorney review all contracts and policies before implementing them. I use a local attorney that specializes in small business management. If you cannot afford legal fees, a great resource is **PrePaid Legal Services™**. I used this service for years and it's an excellent resource for small business owners on a budget. Once you get approval from the attorney, it's time to begin the search for the perfect associate for your business.

There are dozens of books written with guidelines for of hiring the ideal candidate. Many of them have written out questions and ideal answers for interviewing. One of my favorites is **Ask the Right Questions Hire the Best People,** by Ron Fry. This book give numerous scenarios and will give you the skills to attract the best applicants, screen resumes, negotiate salary, offers excellent interview questions, and even tells you what the best answers are. Fry is practical and writes with wit and humor.

The worst thing you can do when interviewing is to hire someone because you like them or because they really need a job. (I Wish I'd Known That!) When hiring, you need to be tough, have high standards and leave your emotions out of the interview process. Afraid? There are head hunters and employee agencies available to you if you are in a position to pay their fees. Otherwise you'll be doing the advertising, interviewing and hiring yourself.

Advertising a job opening used to be as simple as a classified or display ad in your local paper. Today we have so many choices, including newspaper, community magazines and newsletters, job fairs, employment offices, bulletin boards, Craig's List, online services, and even cable TV.

I spoke with hundreds of business owners and would you like to know their favorite medium for finding qualified candidates? None of the above.

Believe it or not 100% of the small business owners that I interviewed stated that they prefer to interview candidates that have been referred to them by other business owners, friends, clients, or community contacts. Think about this, does the perfect person for your open position typically read the classified ads, spend time on Craig's List or surf the help wanted ads on cable? Think of one of your fellow business owners. If they asked you to refer someone for an open position, would you send them just anyone, or would you think carefully and refer someone exceptional?

Before you post an ad in the "Help Wanted" section, shoot an email to your network and let them know what you're looking for.

There are lots of things to keep in mind during an interview. I recommend that you rely on your intuition, as well as considering qualifications. The individual that you select is going to be a reflection of you and your business and perhaps the first person that potential clients meet or speak with on the phone. The candidates attitude is as important as their qualifications. When seeking someone qualified, keep in mind that the right attitude is more important than the right qualifications, especially if these qualifications can be learned on the job.

Once you have chosen the perfect candidate for the job make sure you spend the time to train them well. Quality control issues, lack of motivation, and high turnover rates are frequently due to lack of training and employees not understanding what is required of them.

You can teach an employee skills, but you can't
teach them character or integrity.
Brenda Newberry
The Newberry Group
St. Louis, Missouri

Interviewing and Hiring Tips:

- Outsource if possible, Human Resources, bookkeeping, public relations, etc.
- Consider a Virtual Assistant
- Ask your network to refer excellent candidates
- Use a Professional HR Specialist for employee manuals and company policies & procedures
- Leave your emotions out of the interview
- Have an established training plan for your new staff
- Congratulate yourself on your growth!

If there was one piece of advice I wished I had gotten years ago it would be to hire a Virtual Assistant team. This is the single best thing I've ever done to grow my business while reducing my own workload and stress level. If you have to put it on your credit card initially, do it. Because it frees you up to focus on the things that actually make you money you should quickly be able to cover the cost — and then some.

Stacy Karacostas
Success Team
Seattle, WA

"Too often, we are scattered in our approach to marketing. We try one thing here, another there, and get frustrated when we don't see the results we want. However, when we implement a daily plan of action and use proven strategies that work (and not always the latest fad) on a regular, CONSISTENT basis, that is when we see growth and prosperity."

Cathy Jennings
Weatherproof Networking
Carlisle, Pennsylvania

Chapter Eight

Marketing and Advertising

Effective advertising and publicity can bring you a great deal of new business. Notice that I say effective and not expensive. Your marketing campaign does not have to be expensive, but it does need to be effective.

A good marketing plan will begin before launching your business. Marketing, advertising and public relations are three different ways to promote your business, but they should be designed to compliment one another. If marketing comes easily to you, by all means do it yourself. If it doesn't, you'll want to outsource this crucially important task. Marketing includes all business materials, business cards, brochures, flyers, post cards, direct mail, your website, newsletter, email newsletters and online marketing.

Advertising includes paid or non paid advertising, most often done in printed publications, radio, TV, billboards, and online.

Public Relations, sometimes referred to as community relations or PR, is media or community coverage of you or your business that you do not pay for. Public Relations is so important that I have devoted an entire chapter to it.

Marketing materials need to be professional, and professionally designed. I cringe when someone hands me a business card that is obviously printed on their ink jet home, or worse, one of the "free" business cards offered online that has not been properly typeset or designed. (tip: you can delete their name off the back of the card before printing) That was trendy in the 1990's when these options were brand new, but now it screams I AM A HOME BASED BUSINESS! It makes your business appear new, hobby-like, and not established. Professional printing is so affordable now, even in color, so don't skimp here.

You should have a professional logo or a professional looking logo. Its not acceptable to use clip art for a logo because you want the logo to be unique to you. Professional logo design can take months, because of research and development, but I have never gone that route. I have started all three of my businesses almost as an impulse, and I am not patient enough to wait the several months for research and development.

In each case, I came up with the idea on of how I wanted my logo to look, gave my ideas to a professional graphic artist and requested a quote. After spending years in the publishing business, I'm very good at communicating my needs to a graphic artist. Usually they can get my work done in about an hour, with just a few minor changes after the first submission, so I ask them for an hourly rate. Typically, I pay between $65-$150 for my completed logos. These fees will vary by location and by the expertise of the person you are working with. If you want a logo design that includes research and development, expect to pay up to $5,000 for this service.

Don't just hire any designer. Review their portfolio before you hire them. If it doesn't feel like a good match to you, keep looking.

When you receive your completed logo, be sure you save it on a disc as well as a jump drive. Also email it to yourself to an account that will always be accessible, such as Yahoo or Google, in case something should happen to your computer. With a Yahoo or Google account, you can log into your email from any computer in the world to access your files.

Be sure that your new logo appears on all of your marketing materials with your tag line. Your tag line is a shortened version of your mission statement. People should be able to look at your logo, read your tag line and immediately know what you do and what you have to   offer. If you find that you are always being asked, "What is that?", or, "What exactly is it that you do?", your information isn't clear enough. Tag lines should be short and sweet, about 5-7 words.

For example, my women's organization is Pittsburgh Professional Women. Our mission is to be a resource for business women. We support and empower business women through workshops, seminars and networking. Our tag line is:

We Help Business Women Succeed.

"Pittsburgh Professional Women...what is that?"
"We help business women succeed."
The replies are usually: "Can you help me?" or
"That sounds great, how do I sign up?"

Do you have a tag line? Here are some that have created lasting impressions:

- Just Do It!! (1988)
- We Try Harder (1962)
- Where's the Beef? (1984)
- Don't Leave Home Without It (1975) and
- Melts in Your Mouth, Not in Your Hands (1954!)

A good tagline will have less than seven words and be catchy and easy to remember.

Along with your logo and tag line, all of your marketing material need to have your contact information on each page of each piece. If you have a tri fold mailer or brochure, it needs to be on the front and back. Include your contact name, because that makes you more approachable than just a business name. Include your photo, especially if you are a consultant, coach, or in any service industry.

I have a friend, Susan Lieber, who owns a popular Professional Organizing Business called "**Leave it to Lieber**". Susan kids about having to get along well with her clients, "I'm in people's underwear drawers," she says. "People have to like me to work with me." If you work in an industry that is relationship based, include your photo, with a nice friendly smile. Your materials will stand out above your competition.

Finally, your marketing materials need to be bright, attractive and with easy to read text in font that is at least 12 points. Businesses often want to share too much information in their brochures and flyers, shrinking the fonts to very small sizes. Remember that the majority of people skim these materials. (No one will read and dissect the information like you do.)

Try to remember that the purpose of your marketing material is not to answer each and every question but to make the people want to call you and learn more about what you have to offer. When you get them to call you, then YOU can answer their questions and let them know why you are the best person for the job.

Think about the clients you work with now. What are the top three problems that you solve for them? This would be the information you'd share in your marketing materials. The rest of the information, such as your prices, policies, procedures, and experience can be given later.

Marketing Tips:

- What you do needs to be clearly identified and easy to understand. Avoid industry lingo or abbreviations that people outside of your industry wouldn't understand.
- Use bright and consistent colors and easy to read fonts. You don't want people having to find their glasses to be able to read your phone number.
- Have a professional photo of yourself to use on your marketing materials. If you work with a team, have a photo of everyone in your office for your website and brochure. People like to know who they're working with and it helps to create a personal relationship.
- Avoid having materials that look home made..
- Don't print 5,000 of anything. Your marketing focus may change, or you may find a typo and will be stuck with materials that can't be used.
- Use the front and back of your business card. Some businesses put their mission statement on the back of their cards, some list their website(s) and some include a helpful tip or a call to action, such as a coupon or a special offer.
- Don't be afraid to change and update your marketing materials and your website often. You want your materials to always be fresh and interesting.

As soon as your marketing materials are ready, you can begin with ads. Advertising can be expensive so avoid long term advertising contracts, or any form of advertising that is not proven to be successful in your industry. Don't be afraid to ask questions and expect written proof of any sales pitch. Try to use advertising that can be tracked, so you can measure the effectiveness of each campaign.

I spent years in print advertising, and for some companies it's very effective. For others, its not the best choice. This is a time to get input from other professionals and check with others in your industry to learn what works and doesn't work. Do not fall prey to enthusiastic advertising salespeople. They can provide you with lots of facts and figures but they are not paying your advertising bill.

My first year in business, I handled publicity for an upscale spa that spent tens of thousands of dollars on billboard advertising, with no return on their dollars that they could track. They let their sales rep know that the billboard wasn't working as expected. She suggested a bus station banner that is enclosed between glass at the bench, where people sit as they wait for the bus. The owners of the spa were not thrilled, in fact they were offended. They wanted their beautiful upscale ads to be plastered on billboards in upscale communities in the suburbs, not hanging on bus station benches. They reluctantly agreed to give it a try and within two weeks saw a dramatic increase in walk in traffic.

After a few months they realized that they had been targeting the wrong market. They were getting a   great response on their bus station billboard from women who lived and worked in the neighborhood and came in for spa appointments before and after work. They have a permanent ad there now, and have discontinued all billboards that are further than five miles from their spa's location.

I have a friend, **Vicki Jones**, who owns a very successful weight loss business, **The Pennsylvania Center for Health & Nutrition.** This type of business traditionally pulls a lot of clients from newspaper and magazine ads, so she budgeted over $20,000 in her first years budget for print ads.

The first six months were disappointing and she received very few calls on her ads, despite the fact that they were well designed, colorful and had a great call-in offer. She was also targeting publications that were read by professional women, moms, and brides to be — her target audience.

Vicki received lots of calls, but few turned into clients. She decided to try a large billboard, but the investment was more than she was comfortable with, so she spent a week driving around and looking at billboards in town because she could only afford one, and it had to work. She chose a billboard that was in a part of town where people lived and worked, was near a college and a hospital. It was at the top of a hill where three roads came together and there was a red light at the top of the hill. She used the same ad that had been running in the magazines with a large photo, a little writing and her phone number in a large easy to read font. Within two weeks she got more clients from that billboard ad than she had received in six months of print advertising. Why? Who knows...but now she maintains three billboards and that's the only advertising she does, because it works for her business.

Other clients I work with swear by direct mail. I wouldn't use it; who hires a publicist by direct mail? If it works for you, use it. Radio advertising works well for some industries, especially entertainment. I know chiropractors who wouldn't part with their radio ads, and will never spend another dollar on print advertising.

Another great tool is online pay per click ads. This can work very well if you have someone who knows what they're doing. What I like about these ad campaigns is that you target to se-lected regions and can change them instantly.

Email news campaigns are a necessity for all businesses. Your setup should compliment your other materials. Remember that an email newsletter works better as a resource rather than an advertisement. If you begin to ding your entire address book on a weekly or monthly basis with "buy now" or "on sale this week" you'll find your emails are deleted. Instead, offer a weekly or monthly resource for your ideal clients. These are more likely to be appreciated, saved and forwarded.

Advertising can be very expensive, so you want to plan ahead, do research and get started preferably before opening your doors. If you're on a budget, ask the ad sales reps to call you with specials and last minute price cuts. Don't throw money at ad reps and expect them to do the best job for you. It's not as important to them as it is to you. You need to be very involved with this aspect of your business, or hire someone who has very high standards and understands your mission.

Don't make your advertising difficult. There are basically three tools in marketing yourself and your business:

1. **Tell people** about your business (networking, business cards, email newsletter, brochures, website, public speaking, etc.)
2. **Pay someone** to tell people about your business (paid advertising) or
3. **Have other people tell** the world about your business for free (public relations)

"Keep these three marketing tools on your radar at all times....and the word will get out about you"
Beth Caldwell, Author and Publicity Expert
Pittsburgh, PA

Advertising Tips:

- Find out what works for others in your industry; don't waste your time and money re-learning lessons already learned
- Be polite to ad reps, they can help you and will often offer you discounts close to deadlines, however don't fall for high pressured advertising sales tactics. Decide what you need from advertising and stick to it when dealing with ad reps. You can always revise your rules, but do it on your own, not by being pressured.
- If you plan to do a lot of advertising, consider this when applying for your startup loan.
- Before placing an ad, ask yourself, "Would I answer this ad?", "Would I look here for this service?"
- Don't agree to an expensive ad if you can't afford it. Find an alternative rather than go into debt.
- Take advantage of online marketing, e-zines, and email news campaigns as a compliment to your marketing materials.

Your aim when writing a press release is to get free publicity in or one or a number of different mediums. Any time you can get some free coverage from your local media, it's worth your while.

Brad Sugars
Founder, ActionCoach
Las Vegas, Nevada

Chapter Nine

Creating a Public Relations Plan
for Your Business

Everyone wants publicity! And why not? Publicity is when other people tell the world about your business for FREE. It's the best kind of advertising. Everyone in every type of business should have a publicity plan, but not everyone needs to hire a full time publicist. The toughest part of having a plan is actually creating it. Implementing the plan is easy.

BEFORE you start contacting media, you need to be ready for them to contact you. Nothing is more frustrating to a reporter or producer than being on deadline and calling someone who is a supposed professional, but doesn't have her professional act together.

On the other hand, don't wait until your media kit is PERFECT, because your marketing materials and media information should be constantly updated and improved.

Imagine if your local TV news station were doing a feature story on your industry. Would they know to contact YOU as a business leader to interview you for the piece? If the answer is NO, then its time to create a plan to get the word out about you and your wonderful business or service.

Here is what you <u>must</u> have to be ready for PR:

- Business cards
- Flyer or brochure in printed and electronic form
- Professional photo (ideally more than one shot)
- Professional bio

Here is what would be very nice to have:

- Professional looking website
- Copies of articles that you've written
- Personal and professional recommendations,
- A listing of your awards and accomplishments
- Electronic samples of your voice or video presentation (1 minute, 3 minute, 15minute)
- Several versions of your photo in high and low resolution, some in color, and some in black and white, in a variety of poses and outfits.

Having all of the items on this list is a complete Media Kit, and is ideal, but depending on your business, you may not need all of this. If you do have articles, etc, you should have them available in printed form as well as digital, for a quick and easy email.

Good Media Kit Examples:

www.EleanorSchano.com   see "meet Eleanor" &"media"
www.TheGiftTherapist.com   see "media "
www.clearly-speaking.com   see "media" under "resources"
www.IncredibleMessages.com see "for meeting planners"
www.BornSuccessful.com   see "Press"

Are you at a place in your business where you have no interviews, articles or recordings? That's ok. You can add them when you get them, or you can create your own media for now, and replace it later with actual media. Here are some ideas to do that:

- Schedule yourself for public speaking at the library, community center or Chamber of Commerce
- Use copies of your own email newsletter and announcements
- Write some articles for your ezine, a community or professional newsletter, or for a fellow business owner
- Arrange to do a recorded teleseminar or podcast with a fellow business owner. Take turns interviewing one another to provide the recording for your websites.

Get creative, check your files and you will find that you can pull together a professional media kit in no time!

Publicity Tip:
Host a joint community event with another business owner that compliments your business, for example a travel agent with a bridal planner, a business writer with a web developer, etc. This is what I call "EventWorking" and it's a great way to generate community publicity.
Beth Caldwell
Publicity Expert
Pittsburgh, Pennsylvania

Before creating your plan, you need to understand the process of media coverage. Naturally there are exceptions, but here is the typical process of obtaining effective media coverage. Typically a publicity story works its way from one of the first four options up through the others:

- Online

- Trade or Alumni Magazine

- Community Newspaper or Magazine

- Local Newspaper

- Radio

- Local TV

- Regional TV

- National TV

- National Magazine

With this in mind, you can begin to create your personal publicity list. Your list should include between 5 and 25 media contacts, depending on your type of business. Remember, this is not a one time task. You need to be always updating and improving your list. Currently email is the preferred contact method for most reporters. However, do yourself a favor and create a list with complete contact information.

Include the following in your publicity list:

- Local newspapers and magazines-reporters in the correct department

- Chamber, membership, and alumni organizations and publications

- Regional newspapers and magazines

- Bloggers of well read, well respected blogs with integrity, that directly relate to your subject

- Local radio producers

- Local TV producers

- Regional and national magazines if they are specific to your industry

- Online social networking groups that you are active in including blogging groups, Yahoo, Google, Facebook, Twitter, LinkedIn, Plaxo, etc.
  Tip: Include the passwords and logins for these re sources right on your publicity list, so this task can be easily outsourced when you're ready.

- Anyone else that you can think of who is genuinely interested in your business, your clients, your product and/ or service and its effect on the region or community.

Now that you have your list, decide how often you'll be sending your press releases and announcements. Does your business operate seasonally? Is it a year round business? Are there highs and lows? Consider this when creating your plan. This is how you start.

I recommend that you plan more PR on your less busy months. On your really busy months implement a simple plan. Once you have your marketing materials in order, you will be ready to take advantage of a PR opportunity whenever something happens of interest in the news. Simple press releases are not the only way to generate interest. I also use announcements, eventworking, and tip sheets.

Announcements are a simpler form of communication than a formal press release. A tip sheet can be great as a filler for a magazine or newspaper, particularly if your tips tie to current news. For example, "How to plan a wedding on a budget" or "Five ideas for saving energy this winter".

Eventworking is a form of community relations, something that I started doing years ago, when I was on a very tight budget. Eventworking is what I call events that have no purpose at all, but to do something nice for the community or your clients. As the host, you become known in the community for who you are and what you do. An event such as this is NOT the place to sell, its simply an event that you host with your company name and pride. Yes, you can talk about your business there, have your logo everywhere, have a great program with information on you and what you do, but the event is the main focus. My clients host fundraisers, workshops, networking meetings, health fairs, family fun days, community events, etc.

Tips for sending press releases:

- Always be polite and not pushy or aggressive
- Do not send out mass releases. Personalize each one individually or through a mail-merge.
- Begin with a comment or compliment, not a request. Be genuine. Avoid name dropping.
- Avoid sending files as attachments unless asked. When you do send a file, avoid using obsolete or obscure programs that the receiver may not be able to view. The best thing to do is copy and paste your text right into the body of the email. Let them know that a PDF is available as well as photos.
- Do follow up with a phone call, and leave a brief, concise message. Let them know that you are following up to an email that you sent, and the date and time you sent it.. Give your phone number, speak slowly and clearly and repeat the phone number.

If you haven't heard back from the reporter after 3 emails or 3 calls, chances are, it's not a good fit.. Don't get discouraged. The best thing you can be is a resource to a reporter, and offer them items of interest that is of value to their readership.

People often say to me, "Beth, I have my list but WHAT do I tell them, what should I write about?" Remember this isn't about what people can buy from you. It's about how you can help. Consider these questions:

- What are the five questions/requests that you are asked most often?

- When you've done work for a client, what specifically do they thank you the most for?

- What problems do you solve?

- What is it that you know, have and do that can't be found anywhere else?

- What are you an expert at/in?

- What are you a specialist at/in?

Other reasons to write a press release:

- An award, received by you, your staff, or a client
- A connection with today's news or hot topic
- A celebration or a day in history
- A heartfelt story or good news
- An interesting client that you work with
- Results from a poll — either one you've created or one done by another company or organization.

For a free report called "100 Reasons to Write a Press Release" visit **www.PublicRelationSensation.com** and click on *"Free Reports"*

Sample Formal Press Release

For Immediate Release

Date: month, date, year
Pittsburgh, PA, USA
Contact: Beth Caldwell   412.202.6983

Local Business Woman wins National Award
from Startup Nation!

First paragraph about the award

Second paragraph about the winner and their business

Brief third paragraph with a notable quote and contact
information

For more information contact:

Business Owner Name
Phone Number
Website & Email

###

Sample Formal Announcement

ANNOUNCEMENT!
Month and Year

Contact: Beth Caldwell   412.202.6983

Local Business Owner is Spreading the Warmth this Winter by Collecting Blankets for Homeless Shelter

In the first paragraph list the number of homeless people and how many shelters are in the community.

Second paragraph is about the collection of blankets

Third paragraph insert a quote from business owner, details for drop off, hours, and location.

For more information contact:

Business Owner Name
Phone Number
Website & Email

###

Informal Press Tip

After you've been doing some networking and publicity, you will begin to create a relationship with your local press. At this time, you can be more informal with your press contacts. For example, here is an email that I sent to a local newspaper editor recently:

Hi Peg,

Hope all is well. I was at a chamber meeting last night and thought you'd want to know that Peggy Fayfich is now putting together retreats for businesswomen. She is capitalizing on the down economy by offering the larger businesses an affordable option for business retreats right here at home.

I thought this would be a perfect story for your "business owner in the news' section. Have you met Peggy? Her website is www.strategic-retreats.com. I hope this is a good lead for you!

Beth Caldwell
412.202.6983

Informal Press Announcement

Hi Betsy,

This year I'm on the committee for the National WEDO Tour, (Women's Economic Develop Outreach). This is the ninth consecutive year that WEDO has been empowering business women in our region.

This conference meets in more than fifteen cities across the United States on October 17th. All of the cities and more than 800 business women will be connected via live streaming video.

I know you'll want to be there to cover the event, so mark your calendar! Below is a copy of the flyer. Let me know if you'd like me to email or mail you with the PDF invitation or photos of the panelists.

Have a great day,

Beth Caldwell
412.202.6983

Imagine the worst possible thing that can happen, and plan for it. At some point, you WILL have something bad happen, and you need to have a plan in place to deal with it when it comes along. Planning ahead is absolutely up to you and there really should be no excuses for losing client or company files

Alyssa Lang
Hybrid Photography
El Cajon, CA

Chapter Ten

Preparing for a Crisis

One of the most costly mistakes you can make is not preparing for a crisis. Many of us are so busy running our companies that we don't take the time to create a plan or a system "in case of emergency". Emergencies or crisis can take many forms, it could be something as simple as a power outage in your neighborhood, and as drastic as a serious illness for you or a family member, a natural disaster or a fire. Even if you don't live in an area where tornados or hurricanes frequent, you can still find yourself a victim of a natural disaster.

I was running a successful community publishing business in 2005 when Hurricane Katrina hit New Orleans. I didn't realize at the time how much this hurricane would affect my life and my income. Western Pennsylvania is thousands of miles away from Louisiana, but the effects of the disaster reached for miles.

Among other resources, the price of gasoline, paper and ink skyrocketed. My expenses doubled between September and October. By January they had more than tripled, turning my lucrative home based business into an expensive hobby. Having no way to control the cost of these necessities I had a tough decision to make. I had been cutting costs in every way I could think of. When delivery people quit, I didn't replace them, I took over the routes myself. I began driving to the printer for pickups to save on the fees of delivery trucks and fuel surcharges, but this wore on my personal expenses, not to mention my car and my limited number of waking hours.

Sadly, most of my advertisers were also entrepreneurs or small businesses struggling with increased expenses and decreasing salaries. In March of 2006 I made the difficult decision to sell the business and move into public relations.

I put the printed resources online and moved into the PR field almost effortlessly. At this time most of my regular advertisers could no longer afford to place ads, but they did need public relations.

It was a tough decision but looking back, I realized if I had not been so emotionally attached to my business, selling would have been an easier choice. I got some great advice that really put things into perspective from **Sue Malone**, CEO of **Strategies for Small Business**. She told me that if we could just look at our business like men, decisions would be a lot easier to make.

Looking at my balance sheet, selling was the only decision that made sense financially and for the benefit of my own personal wellness. Its tough to be exhausted, but broke and exhausted just doesn't make any sense, does it?

You must have a plan B. Many business owners do not have a retirement plan because their business is their retirement plan. They plan to work until they're tired of working, sell the business and live off of the sale for the rest of their lives. It's a great idea, but not a secure way to plan for retirement.

The past four decades have shown tremendous achievements in industry. This morning I was speaking with a realtor who was on the internet researching comparable homes for a listing.

The first time I sold my own house (not too long ago), this research was a tedious process done by hand using very large books that were printed monthly. Looking through large news-print books is not practical anymore with the instant information available online. Do you think the person who owned the business that printed those books was able to sell to fund retirement? Not likely.

What about someone who owned a thriving mortgage business before 2007? Very few of those businesses still exist, but many of those business owners are still paying the loans that started their businesses.

Unless you are in the medical, health or funeral business, there is a good chance that the demand for your services will change before you retire, so please have an alternate plan for retirement. Work with a qualified financial planner, accountant, attorney and insurance person to ensure that you have investments other than in your own business, you have retirement funding coming from more than one source, and that less than 50% of your current business is part of your retirement plan.

Review your plan annually. It's human nature to procrastinate when planning for the worst, but when a crisis occurs to someone who has made preparations in advance, the crisis will rarely turn into a life changing tragedy.

Here are some ways that you can be prepared if your business encounters a crisis:

- Know what your company is worth and have it insured for that value, plus replacement costs. If you are in a partnership, have a buy-sell agreement that is funded and prepared by an attorney See a qualified business insurance agent for strategies. Your company value should be appraised by a CPA who is certified to determine business values.

- Have a succession plan that all key people are aware of. A succession plan is a plan that clearly states who will run the business if you are unable to. This can be due to a short term illness, a minor accident, personal leave, or even international travel. Having a plan in place will alleviate issues arising, delays in service and loss of clients. The plan needs to be in writing, clearly stated and easy to locate in your absence. Update this plan quarterly or annually. Having a plan will keep the staff and clients from becoming uneasy in your absence.

- Don't foolishly assume that bad things will never happen to you. Most of us intend to live long and healthy lives, but anyone can have an accident or health issue, including you, your top sales person, your assistant who knows how everything runs in the business, or a friend or family member.

- Have an insurance plan that will protect you, your key people and your business. A good insurance plan can prevent a business or personal bankruptcy.

- Don't use your business to fund your retirement

- Have a replacement income, whether it's a side business, affiliate income, income generated from sitting on an advisory board, speaking engagements, or private consulting. When you earn these additional monies, place them directly into your retirement, or if you can't afford to put all of the money away, put a designated percentage. The sooner you get started, the sooner your replacement income will grow.

- Diversify your investments. Keeping all of your money invested in just your business is too risky and you may wind up working far past retirement in order to make ends meet.

We can weather tough economic times, as long as we've planned ahead.
Susan Wilson Solovic
Author and CEO of SBTV
St. Louis, Missouri

Without you, this business would not have started, and if you don't keep putting your vital, fresh energy into it, it will come to a grinding halt. And so, we can't stress enough how important it is to treat yourself like you would an indispensable staff person.
Lauren Bacon & Emira Mears
Co-authors of : The Boss of You, Everything a Woman Needs to Know to Start, Run and Maintain Her Own Business.
Vancouver, BC

Chapter Eleven

Spreading Yourself Too Thin

One of the best things about a successful business owner is that they are dedicated to their business 24/7. Great for business, not so great for the business owner.

As a business mentor and coach, I work with both men and women and usually it's the women who struggle with work obsession and imbalance between family and career. Men seem to be able to separate work and their personal lives more easily than women do.

Often when working with women, I see that they treat their businesses like their babies, nurturing, feeding, supporting without a break, seven days a week, twenty four hours a day. Yes, I am guilty of this activity but the good news is that once you recognize and become aware of this, its much easier to make adjustments.

Think about when you began your business. I don't imagine that you envisioned yourself working hard, day in and out without a break, being the president, admin, chief marketer, publicist, accountant, personnel manager, customer service manager, and the janitor. It's more likely that you decided to go into business for personal and financial freedom and to be in control of your schedule. Think about it — does your business work for you, or do you work for your business? Who is the owner, you or the business?

If you are guilty of spreading yourself too thin, like many of us are, don't be too hard on yourself. I think it's a part of the growing process from becoming a business owner to someone who runs a business.

The first thing that I recommend is that you limit email and telephone interruptions, especially during your power hours, when you are most focused on your current projects. This is a challenge for me. As a publicist, I have to be really in tune with what is going on in the world. It's important that I see news headlines so that I can take advantage of publicity opportunities for my clients. To compensate, I have learned to limit all unnecessary emails, especially social networking announcements, shopping and travel deals, etc.

Secondly, use one datebook and keep it in sync and updated at all times. For many women this is their sanity. Schedule your family priorities and your money making business activities first, and everything else fits around that. Make sure that you are not overbooking yourself and that you allow enough time between clients to complete work. Schedule office days, so that if you do get behind, you have pre-scheduled time to catch up. Schedule your days off.

I take a week off every month that has five weeks. I don't always take five in a row, but I do go in and block off five days throughout the month as a vacation day. I haven't always done this, and if I forget to block off days, the month goes by and I have missed out on time off.

Its tough in any business to keep balance, whether you own a business or work for someone else it seems like we are all over committed these days. There are lots of books and programs that list do's and don'ts, but here is my simple advice for you:

you: Decide what is most important to you, honor it, and be flexible.

There is no "one size fits all" advice for creating balance in your life. We all have different priorities and are at different stages of life. Some of you have small children at home, some of you don't have children, and some of you have grandchildren. The demands on our lives change as our lives do. When my boys were little, I worked during nap times, two evenings a week with the help of a babysitter, and at night after they went to bed. I didn't watch any TV in the 90's, but I was able to honor what was most important in my life at that time.

Now, that my sons are teenagers, they don't mind having me nearby, but most of the time they prefer to be independent. A normal progression, and just how teenagers should be.

Last fall I moved out of my home office and now I am located about ten minutes away. Now I work around their schedules. I leave after they are gone, come home after school, and do some work from home in the evenings. I can work from home if someone is sick. This system seems to be working very well for us, and when life changes, we'll adjust.

What is most important to you right now in your life? If you are single, it may be your business and growing your income. For some of us spending time with our family, our parents, our pets or a cause is important right now. If you are a mom, it is perfectly fine if what's most important to you is being at home for your kids. Don't ever feel guilty for that. You can have a successful business and be a great parent. Remember that you can do it all, but you don't have to do it all at the same time. Honor what is important to you by your actions, and be flexible when necessary, as a business owner, you need to be.

I try very hard to never use my cell phone for business when I'm with my family. I haven't always done this. I am guilty of visiting my parents and sitting in the driveway for ten minutes after the kids got out of the car because I was on the phone with a client.

A few months ago, I accidentally put my cell phone into the washer with a load of clothes. The cell phone came out very clean and shiny, but it didn't work. It took me about two weeks to get a new one and during that time I learned a really important lesson...its okay not to be available all the time.

I live ten minutes from my office. All of my clients have my cell phone number, and for a while they were all calling me all the time. I was really stressed because I was always on the phone and always available. When I was without my cell phone, I learned that there is no emergency in public relations or business coaching that will happen while I'm on my way home from work.

If my cell phone rings while I am driving, or in a meeting, or with my family, I let the voice mail pick up. In my line of work there are urgent deadlines, but no emergencies. If I am not at work or in my home office, I am at the grocery store, spending time with my family, at a soccer game, or on a date, and I have learned that it's ok to call people back.

I'd like to take a moment to discuss Blackberries and iPhones. These smart phones have the ability to turn people into email and text addicts! It's very frustrating to be in a meeting with someone who is constantly checking their emails and texting. if you have a Blackberry or an iPhone, turn it off when you are in an important meeting, and especially when you're with your family. You can't give your full attention to a business matter when you are doing something else. Have you noticed that if you are constantly multi tasking you are not really doing anything well? If you can, turn off the noisy notifications and vibrations and YOU be in charge of when you check the messages, texts, and emails.

Remember, these technology tools were created to make life easier, NOT more hectic and stressful. Don't be owned by your technology. Use it wisely.

All of the other advice on burnout is good too, things like get adequate sleep each night, eat regular meals, take time to breathe deeply and get away from your desk...but you are all smart business owners, you don't need me to tell you that!

I admit -- I was once guilty of working while attending parties and on date night..but I've stopped "going back to work" once I put my kids to bed, so no more researching and responding to emails at 2 o'clock in the morning. No longer do I take work to my daughter's volleyball games and social gatherings with friends.

Donna L. Johnson
Public Speaker & Business Coach

Everyone Needs Goals!

Sarah Jayne   Louie B

My Goals: My Goals:
More Yard Time   Find Snack Storage
Less Leash Time   Lose 2 Pounds
                              (vets orders)

Compliments of Lisa Spahr
Life Coach & Author
www.LisaSpahr.com

Chapter Twelve

Goal Setting For Success

Recently I attended a holiday brunch with about 12 business professionals, all of them leaders in their fields. Always the social instigator, I asked the group, "Who wants to share their business goals for the new year?" I was genuinely surprised that no one at the table had considered goal setting for their business. I thought everyone did that. I began to inquire and learned that only about 20% of my business contacts set regular goals for themselves. (Now you know the topic of my next business workshop).

I have a great friend, Lisa Spahr, who is a life coach and an author. I attended a seminar of hers where she talked about business and life goals. She told us that everyone in her family has goals, even the dogs, and they post their goals on the refrigerator so everyone in the family becomes supportive. Since that talk, I've been speaking to my sons about their goals, and its been a great experience to watch them set and achieve goals as teens.

How will we know what to do and what's next if we don't have goals? Goals give us direction and something to focus on. I encourage you to take some time to really think about where you want to go in your life and your business. It's a great idea to have goals in all areas of your life: personal, career, family, spiritual and health. It's also ok if you don't achieve each goal you set, because the key to your success is the progress you make.

The way that you set, record and track your goal is as individualized as the way you keep your planner. You have to use what works best for you. As a busy mom and business owner, I have learned if you don't schedule it, it doesn't get done. It's not very effective if you just set your goals once a year in January and then don't review your goals until the next year. Depending on how lofty your goals are, schedule a regular time in your calendar to review and refine your goals. You can write this in your calendar for Sunday evenings, Monday Mornings or Friday afternoons. If once a week is too much, try the last day of the month.

Goals also have to be practical and be broken down into manageable steps. For example, a massage therapist who is seeing about 18 clients a week and earning 26,000 a year may have a goal to double her income. If she says, "My goal is to double my income in the next six months.", I'd reply back to her, That's a great idea...how will you do that?" Just saying it doesn't make it happen. She needs to break this down into smaller, more achievable statements that can be measured.

Often I coach business women who are at a crossroads. They need to start making money now, or they have to get a real job. Here are some action steps that can help anyone increase clients and sales in a short time period:

- I will eliminate large openings in my calendar between appointments. I will choose when I work and book appointments according to my designated schedule. I can achieve this by having specific openings in my calendar when clients call.

- I will increase my clients from 18 per week to 25 per week within three months. I can achieve this by asking for referrals, networking, calling on my referral partners, and reminding my network of the benefits of working with me.

- I will begin increasing my referrals and bookings by systematically building my contact list, offering exceptional customer service, asking for referrals, and following up consistently. I will create a 12 month publicity plan and send one item a month to local media.

- I will begin sending my newsletter monthly with tips and resources for my client base.

- I will attend 4 networking events a month, become active with my chamber, and add at least ten new subscribers each month to receive my newsletter.

- I will conscientiously up-sell to all clients, offering add-on services, gift certificates, etc.

- I will begin sending a thank you note for all referrals and create a client appreciation program.

- I will participate in community events that appeal to my ideal client.

These eight strategies will create a synergy to increase sales and income. If one or more of them are not embraced 100%, the others will still work. Don't be upset if you don't get to all 8 steps right away, because the strategies that you do act on will increase sales and business, and help you to achieve your goal.

For thirteen years, I was an Independent Beauty Consultant with Mary Kay Cosmetics. My training with Mary Kay was phenomenal. It was there that I learned about goal setting and that goals need to be **SMART:**

S   Specific
M   Measurable
A   Attainable
R   Realistic
T   Timely

Specific means that it can't be general. "I will double my income" is too general. "I will increase by client base by 25 by the end of next month", is specific. **Measurable** means that you have to be able to see the results — like a number of sales, a dollar amount, a number of clients, etc. **Attainable** means realistic. Attaining 100 new clients in thirty days may not be **Realistic. Timely** means that you give yourself a short but reasonable amount of time to reach your goal. Have you ever tried to lose weight for a special event? If the event is more than a year off, then saying I want to lose 20 pounds for my reunion next June doesn't make you work too hard, but I want to lose 20 pounds for my reunion in three months requires action NOW.

A good goal will be realistic and attainable but still make you stretch to achieve it. Mary Kay used to tell us, "Give yourself something to work toward, constantly. A good goal is like a strenuous exercise — it makes you stretch."

Once you set some goals, I encourage you to share them with your support system. It's important that your family know about your goals. If you have children and you share your goals with them you are doing two things:

- You are modeling a great life skill.
- You are showing them what you achieve when you are not at home. This can be very helpful for little ones who hate the time you spend away from home.

Sharing goals with your family can also backfire. Sometimes the ones we love the most are the ones who will point out our shortcomings, or feel free to criticize us. Besides family, have someone in your life to help empower and support you in business. For me, that's my Mastermind Group.

Mastermind Groups are a great way to set and achieve goals. I belong to a mastermind group meets twice a month on the first and third Tuesdays. We chose those times because the first week of the month is a great time to begin with your goals, and the third week is good because you still have time before the end of the month. During our meetings, we discuss our business strategies and talk about our goals. This is not a venting session, nor a place for excuses. Each of us takes a turn sharing what happened with our businesses in the past two weeks. We always begin with, "Here is what I accomplished", and end with, "Here is what I am working on now". Our meetings finish with one of us reading back everyone's goals and intentions for the next two weeks. Even though we are friends, we do not discuss family and personal issues during mastermind meetings.

If goal setting is new to you, consider your goals as your roadmap for your business. Often when setting goals, I begin with the future in mind. Ask yourself "where do I want to be in 5 years?" and work backward from that goal. Its easier to achieve something really big when you do it one step at a time.

As your long term goals come closer or even change, you may need to tweak your short term goals. Remember that achieving your goals is a good thing, but they need to work for you. If your vision changes, your goals will change too.

It's very difficult for me to see a woman beating herself up for not achieving something. Often we are trying to achieve things that may not be in our best interest. Please recognize that you are making progress, even when you fail. Have faith in yourself as a woman and as a leader in your field and your community. Always recognize what you've achieved, instead of regretting what you haven't achieved (yet).

Large goals can be achieved by setting mini goals. I want to encourage you to think BIG. Don't limit yourself. Dream about what you can achieve and how you can influence the world around you. Take it one step at a time. I can't wait to see what you achieve!

To live your passionate life, it is important to surround yourself with reminders of what you want. Write down your passions and desires. Don't hide them in your computer or drawer. Post them throughout your home and office.
Keep them visible!
Barb Dull
Principal Owner Incredible Moms
www.incrediblemoms.net

Alone we can be successful,
but together we can be significant.
Rebecca Lamperski
President and CEO of Full Bloom PPC, and author of
Full Bloom; Planting the Seeds of Your Future

Chapter Thirteen

Resources

I hope you will use and refer to this chapter for months and years after reading this book. This is the best part of "Secrets to Success in Business from Women Who've Been There". Here we all share our best resources with you. I am constantly learning and believe that to be successful you need to surround yourself with people who are doing better than you and learn from them! I hope these resources are helpful to you.

We will continue to add and update resources on our website and if you have any, please share!

Keep checking online at **www.IWishIdKnownThat.com** and click on "Resources For Business Women".

Please note: These recommendations may become inaccurate as time passes, so visit the website often for updates and current information. The resources on these pages are recommended with the best of my ability, but I do not accept responsibility for any purchases, business conducted, or relationships created or initiated from this directory. I may receive compensation from some referrals as a "thank you", however, NO company or organization is recommended based on commissions or incentives. * Means that I currently use and love this resource.

Balancing Family & Career

Jennifer Antkowiak, Author and Caregiving Coach
www.JenniferCares.com

Borrowing Money

Community Express Loan Program
www.StrategiesForSmallBusiness.com

Business Development & Personal Coaching

Book Yourself Solid, a book by Michael Port, visit his website for a free chapter www.BookYourselfSolid.com

*The Champions Coaching Series
www.LisaSpahr.com

Donna L Johnson, Motivation & Empowerment
Coaching www.DonnaLJohnson.com

Incredible Moms, Life Coaching for Single Moms by Barb Dull
www.IncredibleMoms.net

*Profit Club, a program through Action Coach Business Coaching is a great mastermind/group coaching program. Visit www.ActionCoach.com to find a coach in your area. Also, read any book written by Brad Sugars, the founder of Action Coaching.

*Women's Economic Development Outreach, a coalition of business experts working in collaboration to provide focused resources that help women owned and managed businesses flourish. www.WE-DO.net

Business Support

Elance.com has quality professionals when you need a job out-sourced quickly, from simple administrative tasks to legal and manufacturing projects

*Evoice and Efax for an extra phone or voice mail line, or to receive faxes directly to your email account
www.evoice.com www.efax.com

*Padgett Business Services for affordable, effective bookkeeping, accounting and payroll services visit
www.smallbizpros.com to locate an office near you

PrePaid Legal Services, Inc. www.PrepaidLegal.com

*QuickBooks — I use Simple Start, a free downloadable version of QuickBooks available for download
www.SimpleStart.com

*Small Business Television Network offers daily business news headlines especially for small business owners and entrepreneurs www.SBTV.com

Graphic Design

*DS Graphics Dan Szwedko has created some of the best business cards I've ever seen, I send all my clients to him
www.dsgraphics.net

Hiring

DLJ & Associates has programs to help you hire the right person for the job as well as fantastic diversity training
www.dljandassociates.com

Leadership

*Leadership International
www.LeadershipInternational.com

Marketing

For clever marketing ideas visit www.MarketingSensation.com

For a free audio CD on marketing your business visit
www.ClientAttraction.com

Get Clients Now! is an excellent book and there are programs offered throughout the US. Visit www.GetCLientsNow.com

Networking & Business Organizations

BNI www.BNI.com

*eWomen www.ewomennetwork.com

Joy of Connecting www.thejoyofconnecting.com

NAFE www.NAFE.com

NAWBO www.NAWBO.org

*Weatherproof Networking, great tips on networking success www.WeatherProofNetworkingBlog.com

The Referral Institute teaches you to create referrals for life www.ReferralInstitute.com

*Zonta International www.zonta.org

Office Organization

Taming The Paper Tiger Software www.thepapertiger.com

Red Lotus Letter, Feng Shui Ezine for Abundant Living Kathryn Weber Master Feng Shui Consultant www.redlotusconsulting.com

Office Space

*Regus Offices Worldwide
www.Regus.com

Publicity/Press Releases

If you haven't heard of Peter Shankman, you don't know what your missing! Visit his website at once and sign up for daily emails from ***HARO*** (Help a Reporter Out). You'll begin receiving notices immediately from reporters who need quotes and interviews. www.HelpaReporter.com
www.Shankman.com

PR Newswire is a press release service especially for small businesses, start-ups, and entrepreneurs www.PRnewswire.com

For clever publicity tips and programs, and lots of   resources, visit www.PublicRelationSensation.com

*Jill Lublin's One Day Crash Course in Publicity
www.JillLublin.com/seminars.php

Publishing & Writing

Author House
www.AuthorHouse.com

InCredible Messages, Bonnie Budzowski
www.incrediblemessages.com

Publishing & Writing

Gina Mazza, Creative Muse and Editor
www.ginamazza.com

St. Lynn's Press
www.stlynnspress.com

Setting Prices

Women's Earning Institute
www.MikelannValterra.com

Shopping Cart Systems

*Authorize.Net®
www.authorize.net

*E-Junkie
www.e-junkie.com

Mal's e-Commerce
www.mals-e.com

Reliance Business Solutions, Diane Bombarra
www.visionpayments.com

Virtual Assistant

**Dynamic Support Solutions
www.DynamicSupportSolutions.com

Website Resources

*2TechDivas for help with online tools and marketing
www.2TechDivas.com

*For help finding available domain names www.nameboy.com

Camtasia helps you to provide high quality web video for pres-
entations an tutorials. Free 30 day trial www.camtasia.com

*Emilie Nottle, Graphic and Web Designer, Online Strategist.
www.zooop-design.com

Web Makeovers, Susan Bluemling, Certified Internet
Webmaster and Master Site Designer
www.web-makeovers.com

New Resources:
visit: www.IWishIdKnownThat.com

INDEX

INDEX

INDEX

INDEX

INDEX

Other Products from BETH CALDWELL:

Beth is the creator of "Monday Morning Mastermind", a very popular mastermind workshop for busy entrepreneurs across the US and Canada. The Mastermind meets by tele-conference every Monday Morning. To learn more visit
www.MondayMorningMastermind.com

Beth is the author of several helpful books for business women:

The Professional Women's Guide to Golf

The Professional Women's Guide to Networking

The Professional Women's Guide to Getting Paid What You're Worth

She offers resources on the following websites:

www.PublicRelationSensation.com
www.MarketingSensation.com
www.IWishI'dKnownThat.com
www.MondayMorningMastermind.com

For a bonus resource, turn the page!

BONUS!
An Excerpt From:
101 REASONS TO WRITE A PRESS RELEASE

1. New employee
2. Promotion
3. Certification
4. Community award
5. Business award
6. New or updated website
7. Company anniversary
8. New product or service
9. Speaking Engagement
10. Poll Results (create your own poll)
11. Company support of a non profit
12. Contest
13. Company Going Green
14. Support of a School Program or Initiative
15. Educational Program
16. Holiday Affiliation
17. This day in History Affiliation
18. Employees on a committee
19. Getting a new client
20. Taking on a new large project
21. Affiliation with a strategic partner
22. Free offer on website
23. Moving to a new location
24. Redecorated store front or office

BONUS!
An Excerpt From:
101 REASONS TO WRITE
A PRESS RELEASE

25. Piggy Back news story
26. Participation in a fair or trade show
27. TV show or media affiliation
28. Sports Team affiliation
29. Upcoming Presentation or Workshop
30. Free Tip Sheet on your Website
31. Announcing a new intern
32. Opportunity to volunteer
33. Completion of a degree or training program
34. Open House
35. Legislation that affects your business
36. Industry Trends
37. Announcement of media coverage
38. Important Guest or Celebrity Visiting
39. Celebrity Endorsement
40. Discount or Rewards Program
41. Thank you letter or recognition from celebrity
42. Trends of other industries that affect your business
43. Adding bi lingual marketing materials
44. Google Ranking

**To Get the Complete Report for FREE, visit
www.PublicRelationSensation.com.**

About the Author

Beth Caldwell owns a public relations firm in Greentree, Pennsylvania. She is a specialist at creating unique publicity and marketing plans for small business owners and entrepreneurs. She is the Executive Director of Pittsburgh Professional Women, a resource organization that supports professional businesswomen with practical and affordable workshops which keep them up to date with the latest tools, resources and technology to help them find success in business. She is also the founder of "Monday Morning Mastermind" a mastermind group for business owners across the United States that meets via teleconference every Monday morning.

A dynamic speaker, Beth presents workshops on entrepreneurship, leadership and business topics all over the US and Canada. She has also written *The Professional Women's Guide to Golf, The Professional Women's Guide to Networking*, and is writing a book on raising a child with autism. The book is called "*Autimism*" and will be published in 2010.

Beth is a single parent and lives with her teenage sons Brian and Kevin in Pittsburgh, Pennsylvania.

Secrets to Success in Business!

Secrets to Success in Business